Alkaline Gree

Delicious Fruit, Veggie
Superfood Smoothie Recipes to
Help You Look and Feel
Amazing (even on a busy
schedule)

By Marta "Wellness" Tuchowska

ISBN: 9781797050461

All information in this book has been carefully researched and checked for factual accuracy. However, the author and publishers make no warranty, expressed or implied, that the information contained herein is appropriate for every individual, situation or purpose, and assume no responsibility for errors or omission. The reader assumes the risk and full responsibility for all actions and the author will not be held liable for any loss or damage, whether consequential, incidental, and special or otherwise, that may result from the information presented in this publication.

The book is not intended to provide medical advice or to take the place of medical advice and treatment from your personal physician. Readers are advised to consult their own doctors or other qualified health professionals regarding the treatment of medical conditions. The author shall not be held liable or responsible for any misunderstanding or misuse of the information contained in this book. The information is not intended to diagnose, treat or cure any disease.

Contents

Part 1: Introduction to Alkaline Green Smoothies

"This is already getting boring," I said to myself while sipping on a plain banana spinach smoothie.

"There must be a better way," I thought.

Now, don't get me wrong.

I certainly don't want anyone to feel bad about making the most classic green smoothie recipe there is- spinach, banana and a bit of water.

It certainly works, especially if you want to use some leftovers.

And we should certainly feel grateful for all we have.

But...when it comes to green smoothies, there is so much more to it. Not only in terms of taste, but also overall ingredient combination.

We don't need to depend on the same recipe over and over again.

What if we get bored with it and because of that we get off track?

There is no limit to how many amazing superfoods we can use to make our green smoothies in a myriad of different ways so that:

-we make smoothies in alignment with our health goals (whether it's weight loss, having more energy or even fighting insomnia)

-we strategically design our smoothies in such a way that we get a ton of miraculous veggies in and they taste incredible

-we take advantage of many, proven , healing herbs.

Talking about herbs and some of the superfoods that some of the recipes of this book call for... Most of them are very easy to find.

That is not a problem.

After talking to many of my readers and clients I came to the conclusion that the main problem is "Yea, I ordered this or that, it's sitting on my kitchen shelf, but I don't really know how to put it all together or I forget about it".

That is why I am writing this book.

I want to show you how "outside the box" your green smoothies can be. So that you feel inspired and empowered knowing that you have a myriad of recipes to pick and choose from.

If you decide to skip a recipe or two, or maybe even more recipes, for whatever reason (taste, ingredients, allergy or other), you will still be in possession of so many tantalizing options.

After reading this book, you will feel empowered to:

-have one delicious green smoothie a day

-practice holistic self-care

-use food as a fuel to help you have more energy

What I really love about the smoothie recipes from this book is that:

-they can be a meal replacement

-they are very easy and quick to make

-they can be made in batches

(For example, I make my smoothies every other day, so if today is Monday and I make my smoothies, I have a serving for today and tomorrow.)

-they inspire you to start adding a myriad of superfoods and herbs too while educating you what is good for what

(I am not a big fan of theory, I prefer mindful, free-of-judgment practice; and the best way to practice is to keep trying out different recipes to see which ones you like.)

-low in sugar and alkaline-forming in their design

If you are new to the alkaline diet, don't worry, later in this chapter I provide a short "alkaline diet crash course" and free access to my Alkaline Wellness VIP Reader Newsletter where you can get free charts and even more recipes and guides to help you on your journey.

My goal as an alkaline diet lover, wellness coach and author is not just to publish some guides hoping you will figure it out.

Since you have invested in this book, I want to go the extra mile and equip you with other free, complimentary resources to make sure you feel empowered and inspired on your wellness quest and that you enjoy every second of it.

Actually, you can go ahead and grab them now.

It's a *Full Alkaline Wellness Toolkit* that consists of three eBooks (including yummy plant-based desserts) and easy to use alkaline-acid charts (beginner friendly). The total value of those books is $67, but you can get them all free of charge by signing up to our newsletter at our private website:

www.HolisticWellnessProject.com/alkaline

Feel free to reply to my first email and say *hi*.

I love connecting with my readers and your questions are always very welcome!

Now, back to Alkaline Green Smoothies...

For now, I will simply mention that smoothies are not just about blending some fruit. We also want to get some veggies in. Smoothies don't have to be sweet. They can. But they don't have to be. In fact, they can also be spicy, sour and even turned into a delicious and super satisfying healing soup.

After publishing one of my first books, "Alkaline Smoothies", I received a ton of emails from readers telling me how much they appreciated the fact that not all the recipes were about sweet smoothies and fruit.

At the same time, the book gave our readers a ton of variety because it wasn't only about the veggie smoothies either.

In the end, balance is the key.

So how is this book different from my other alkaline books?

Well, it takes a different angle in a way that our focus here is on green smoothies.

The goal is to help you add more greens into your diet, and we are using smoothies as a super effective and delicious tool.

I can still remember making my first green smoothies and not really enjoying them. I just had no idea how to really make them in such a way that they tasted good too.

While practice makes perfect, this recipe book is designed as a shortcut on your wellness journey. With this book, you will have it a lot easier than I did in terms of focus, strategy and motivation.

It's basically a book I am writing for my younger self. Something I wish I'd had at the outset of my journey.

Talking of which...

Imagine the feeling of literally jumping out of bed full of energy every morning. No mental fog. Full alertness.

You see...you don't need to depend on caffeine for energy.

Glowing skin and shiny hair are an extra bonus and so is the natural weight loss.

Everyone around you wants to know your secret...

To me that is an Abundance of Holistic Health.

Taking care of your body, mind and soul.

It starts with your mindset and intention. Making that decision:

"I am healthy, it's who I am."

"I take care of my body and mind."

"I focus on the long-term."

"My body is my temple."

From there, commit to a simple wellness goal.

I usually recommend process oriented goals. An example of which can be:

Have one green alkaline smoothie a day.

It's really that simple. Then, set up a time to drink that smoothie.

It can be in the morning, afternoon or both.

Also, what I really love about making smoothies is that you can use smoothie leftovers to make *Alkaline Smoothie Bowls* (I have an entire recipe book on that topic, you will find it on Amazon and on my website HolisticWellnessProject.com/books).

At the end of this book, I have included a few bonus recipes to introduce you to *Alkaline Smoothie Bowls* which is the next step on your journey, after you have familiarized yourself with *Alkaline Green Smoothies.*

The smoothies from this recipe book can be made in different versions and it's entirely up to you.

For example, sometimes I like to make a thick smoothie that is almost like a soup. Sometimes, I like to add more liquid to my smoothie so that it's more like a juice when it comes to its consistency.

Now, since the topic of juicing has come up, let me explain the difference between juicing and smoothies.

Both are awesome by the way. I see lots of ridiculous "fights" in the health and wellness community where people attack one another.

(Something I don't really understand. I always stay away from the drama and it works well for me. Health is also about taking care of our emotions and stress levels. And some individuals are never happy anyway and always looking to attack other people in one way or another, lol.)

That being said- to juice, or to smoothie? That is the question...

Juicing vs Smoothies

The rule is very simple- it all depends on the goal that you have.

For example, juicing must be done the right way. Unfortunately, many people miss that point. It's not their fault at all. There is just so much mis-information out there.

You see, juicing is a fantastic way to boost your energy levels quickly. When you juice, you extract pure juice and there is no fiber and so that allows your digestive system to rest.

Since there is nothing to digest and with juicing you give your body a ton of nutrients, you naturally start experiencing more energy.

However, like I have already mentioned, juicing must be done the right way. For example, if you juice fruit that is high in sugar, you will only cause havoc in your body. In that case, it's better to blend that fruit or eat it in its whole form, without extracting the fiber.

Simple Explanation

That is why, when you juice, it's very important to focus on low-sugar ingredients. Veggies and fruit that are low in sugar.

These are examples of fruits that are low in sugar: lemons, limes, grapefruits, tomatoes, pomegranates.

Because of their low sugar and high mineral content, they are considered alkaline-forming fruits (more on that later in the *Alkaline Diet Crash Course*). Bingo! If you are new to the alkaline diet, that is one of the most important lessons.

Juicing is something I like to add to my diet on a daily basis. (Sometimes every other day if I am pressed for time.)

For example, I juice: grapefruits, a bit of spinach, red bell peppers and a bit of ginger. Beautiful juice for optimal high performance.

The main goal behind my juicing routine is to boost my energy levels and improve digestion. For juicing, I use an Omega juicer which I have been using since 2014. It was the best health investment I have ever made. I remember that when I first decided to order it many of my friends were laughing at me. I felt like an outcast.

Now however, they come to me for advice, because they have seen how much my health and life have transformed.

So, I definitely recommend smart health and wellness investments. While I am not a big fan of fad diets, pills and gadgets, some equipment simply makes sense for long-term wellness success and massive ROI. The health "bank account"!

However, if you are on a tight budget, or perhaps have other reasons not to invest in a professional juicer, that's fine. When I first got started on my health journey, I was using a simple lemon squeezer (to juice lemons, limes and grapefruits) and a simple hand blender to make my smoothies.

It didn't really work well for leafy greens, so eventually I decided to save up for a Vitamix Blender.

But again...it's not that much about tools. It's about your WHY.

The most important thing is to be proactive and to focus on the compound effect aka "be consistent". Now, we are getting off the topic a bit. I always get a bit carried away when talking about Motivation (one of my biggest passions to talk about).

To finish off the topic of juicing for the time being, I would recommend you read my book *Alkaline Juicing*. I also have an amazing article and audio article on my blog (it's focused on *Juicing for Weight Loss*, but the tips I share there can also be applied to juicing for other health goals).

Here's the link to that bonus article:

www.HolisticWellnessProject.com/juicing

Our readers and followers really appreciated the fact that I added a free audio version to this post. So, listen on the go, stay inspired and enjoy!

Smoothies Compared to Juices

With smoothies, the process is a bit different than it is with juicing.

When you blend fruits and veggies to make a smoothie, you are not separating them from their natural fiber.

And so, when you are drinking your smoothie, even if you are using fruit that is higher in sugar, there is a certain limit to how much of a smoothie you can drink because of the high fiber content. You will feel fuller much faster.

People who are watching their blood sugar sometimes prefer blending to juicing because the fiber ensures a slow and steady absorption of sugar into the bloodstream. And we can also focus on blends aka smoothies that use low sugar ingredients anyways.

(Please note, if you suffer from any health condition that requires you to reduce all forms of sugar in your diet, even natural sources coming from fruit, you will need to focus on veggie smoothies or use fruit that is low in sugar- which is how most of the recipes in this book have been designed anyway.)

Smoothies are like a "magic blend" that offers all the benefits of fiber from healing fruits and veggies. Great for your gut and heart health.

I always say that smoothies are easier and faster to make, but it might take a bit longer to go through them.

With juicing, it's the opposite- it's a bit of a process to juice a big bowl of ingredients, especially if you are juicing greens, ginger (yes, I am a crazy woman and I juice ginger), and some fruit. But then, since there is no fiber, you can gulp it down easily. Boom. Done. Energy.

But again, a juice cannot be a meal replacement (unless you are on some kind of a juice fast which is not what we are covering in this book).

Smoothies will make you feel full for longer though.

At the same time, people who can't tolerate too much fiber for whatever reason should focus on juicing (or low fiber, thin smoothies).

Now, I hope that this short comparison has demonstrated that there is no right or wrong. It's a question of focus, goals and what's better for you in a given moment.

Many people use the term "juice" and "smoothie" as if they are the same thing, which can be very confusing for a beginner. (It certainly was for me when I was first getting started on my health and wellness journey.)

But once you have understood what it's all about, and you know what your goal is and what to focus on, with daily consistency you will start unleashing all that hidden natural energy that will help you reach new levels of health, fulfillment and success in your life. That is my goal- to help achieve yours.

Since this is a smoothie book, I want to keep it to the point.

If you want to learn more about juicing, please read the following article on my blog (recipes included).

www.holisticwellnessproject.com/juicing

Treat it as a bonus companion to this book!

My Biggest Why and How to Determine Yours (it really helps stay motivated)

Now, here's a little bit about myself in case it's the first time you are picking up one of Marta's books.

My biggest value in life is health. I know that when I am healthy, and I feel aligned I am truly the best version of myself.

That allows me to focus on helping other people to the best of my ability.

And I can also focus on growing other areas of my life and creating balance.

Now, at thirty-five years old, I feel like I have cracked the code to wellness and wellbeing- on a physical, emotional and mental level. Still, I am on a never-ending quest of learning and practicing which is my biggest passion in life.

One of my health and wellness mentors once told me: never stop learning, the moment you stop, it all ends. And the best way to learn is by doing.

But you see, it wasn't always that way. I have been through lots of pain and suffering due to serious health problems that plagued me for years. Because of that I felt depressed, demotivated and every day was a struggle. I felt so much pain in my body that I would resort to alcohol which of course added to the problem.

Now, looking back at where I was before, I can say I am feeling grateful for that pain and suffering for numerous reasons, such as – I can totally relate to the pain, frustration and discomfort that other people are feeling. That allows me to develop a strong sense of empathy and connection so that I can really help people transition to a healthier, happier and more empowered lifestyle. That passion really keeps me going. Whenever I receive an email from a happy reader who is now on their unique journey of transformation, I feel forever grateful and inspired.

So, you may be wondering what happened to me exactly. What led me to my transformation and what my health story is.

When I was only four years old, I suffered from a severe attack of uveitis.

*"**Uveitis** (pronounced you-vee-EYE-tis) is inflammation of the uvea — the middle layer of the eye that consists of the iris, ciliary body and choroid. **Uveitis** can have many causes, including eye injury and inflammatory diseases."* – from Wikipedia

It's a condition triggered mostly by autoimmune system disorders and manifests as a serious health condition that can even cause blindness.

That was the diagnosis that most doctors would give me back then.

The treatment was very brutal, I even remember getting eye injections during that time, as a kid. I also have a very blurry memory of going to stay at an eye clinic that was located on the other side of the country. Of course, my parents would come and visit me as often as they could, but most of their time was spent back in our home town working very hard to be able to pay for my treatment.

I had been given huge doses of hormone treatments and antibiotics. The doctors were very confused, and it seemed like there was no cure. That was back in the eighties in Poland. Most medicine was not even available for us there.

However, my parents had the courage to keep investigating and found a functional medicine eye doctor who was able to help me by combining traditional medicines with natural ones. An interesting thing is that now he's over ninety years old and still in his health clinic in the mountains! Enjoying vibrant health and helping other people.

Luckily for us, my dad also happened to have an amazing friend and colleague from the UK. That English college of his was very helpful as he managed to find the medication that at that time was not available in my native country.

So that was my first exposure to a holistic approach. Combining standard medicine and scientific research with an integrated approach to health, balance and healing.

I always stress that I am not a fan of some woo-woo or people who totally reject doctors and standard medicine. There are many medications that literally save people's lives. At the same time, the integrated, natural approach focuses on lifestyle change, prevention and stimulating the body's natural healing responses.

Both are awesome when combined the right way, by specialized doctors who also are aware of the holistic approach to healing and health.

Finally, the treatment with that functional medicine doctor helped me and my eyes were healed.

From there, all the memory I have is of my dad picking me up from the clinic. I went back to my home town and started school, and that was when my little brother was born.

As I was leaving that clinic, the doctor told us that the amount of antibiotics and hormones I had been given as a child was something he had never seen before. He said it would take many years to get it all out of my system and that I may be prone to some hormonal imbalances later as I grow up. He also said that any imbalances in my lifestyle may lead to the uveitis manifesting itself again.

I had a normal, peaceful childhood, although I would very often get sick. Same as a teenager. I would be sick several times a year.

But the uveitis did not come back. Until I was twenty-nine.

What a nightmare. When I found out about it from my eye doctor, I felt so depressed. All that vague blurred memory from my childhood got back to my adult life.

I managed to find some courage though. Since I was living abroad, I decided to find a functional medicine eye doctor in my area. *If it doesn't help*, I said to myself, *I will go back to the same clinic in my home country.*

Although... you know, adult life is different, you've got work and bills to pay. So, I decided to look for qualified ophthalmologists locally.

At that time, I was already getting into a heathy lifestyle and was making some big changes in my professional life too. After going through lots of stress because of my pretty unfulfilling work at that time and other personal problems I was facing, I knew I was out of balance. Something was wrong. And that clearly manifested as a disease.

Luckily, I found an amazing international ophthalmologist who also specialized in natural medicine. In fact, she was integrating standard medicine (so necessary to get all the checkups, data, analysis and information) with cleverly designed natural healing.

I followed her treatment and healed my eye in less than three months.

Following her recommendation, I began looking into an anti-inflammatory diet and that led me to discovering the alkaline diet, which I will tell you more about in a second.

At first when I came across it, I felt very skeptical about it and thought it was a fad!

Long story short, in my twenties I wasn't really that healthy.

Partying, low end corporate life, long commutes, drinking, smoking and not eating a clean food, balanced diet.

It was taking its toll on me. That eye disease was a wake-up call.

Prior to that I suffered from another issue and no doctors could help...That issue was low energy levels and constant allergies. It was affecting my performance at work. I had no idea what to do, no idea what to eat.

I remember that there was a period where I would be back from work between six and seven in the evening and immediately go back to bed. And while in bed I could not enjoy quality sleep either, but I felt severe anxiety. Like waking up around 3-4 AM, in severe pain all over my body, scared. I very often cried, feeling hopeless.

Then, the mornings were a nightmare. Alarm clock and overdoing coffee just to keep going. During that time, I could never lose any excess weight, even when I "tried". I just felt so much out of balance and no "conventional wisdom" (count calories, skip this and that, eat low-fat) seemed to work. I remember feeling very frustrated and confused.

However, after discovering the alkaline diet, things began to change. It started off with my medical condition, the uveitis attack, that really motivated me to change my lifestyle.

The whole lifestyle, not just food. The way I lived, thought and also my career. I consciously decided to design my life in such a way that health would be my highest priority. I also knew this:

After I transform and make myself super healthy, strong and energized, I will start sharing and teaching the exact process to other people.

It was a process; the changes didn't come overnight. While transitioning to a healthy lifestyle, many of my old friends would laugh at me because I didn't want to drink with them at the bar.

But that initial holistic health journey also helped me re-align myself with my true-life purpose and meet many other supportive people.

Honestly, everyone is at a different place on their journey and judging other people for their choices is like judging myself from ten years ago so I will leave it here.

My focus is now on 100% empowerment.

The work is still in progress. I am not perfect.

I want to show you that everything is a process and that small decisions lead to a compound effect.

Things don't happen *to* us, they happen *for* us.

One of my indirect mentors (by indirect I mean that we never had a one-on-one interaction and I learned via his books and online courses) Yuri Elkaim, lost all his hair when he was seventeen years old. It happened due to an autoimmune condition.

But eventually that made him decide he was going to get super strong and transform his health with a balanced diet and fitness and help others do the same.

Why am I mentioning all this?

Empowerment. Courage. Motivation.

We all get started somewhere. Never compare yourself to other people, your journey is truly unique!

Looking back, like I said, I am grateful for what happened *to* me because it actually happened *for* me.

My own health issues (like the autoimmune disease that manifested in a uveitis eye attack, low energy levels, anxiety, depression and weight issues too) led me to seek and master holistic solutions.

I found my answers in an integrated lifestyle and "alkaline inspired", clean food diets.

(I am very big on personalized diets, I don't like dogmas or labels, even though it may seem I label myself with "alkaline").

Thanks to that I was able to create HolisticWellnessProject.com and inspire people to live a healthy balanced lifestyle and give them practical tools to do so.

Thanks to inspiration and re-charged energy levels I was able to write numerous health and wellness guides related to the alkaline lifestyle as well as mindfulness and motivation.

Finally, I was able to create an online program AlkalineDietLifestyle.com which allows me to educate and inspire people from all around the world to transition to an alkaline diet in accordance with their needs and personal preference.

I am not saying this to brag.

I simply want to show you how negative can be turned into positive.

And how small, healthy decisions can compound and help you transform on a deeper level.

With vibrant health you can literally do whatever you want, and it will seem like you have more free time, due to more energy levels.

Yes, some people might say that what you do is weird, it happened to me many times. But guess what? Some people will be inspired.

And that is my intention. I want you to inspire those around you. Help them make heathy choices. Not by preaching. By living and sharing.

So, be a holistic leader in your small community. Trust me- people will love it!

OK, enough of motivational talk, I guess you must be on fire right now.

You see, the reason behind me writing my books is not to create a plain and boring "how to" book that gets forgotten in your eBook device or on your bookshelf.

My intention is to really inspire you so that you can use it to transform the way you desire to.

If you are not new to the alkaline diet, feel free to skip this mini sub-chapter and dive straight into the recipes.

PART 2 Alkaline Diet Crash Course - Understand the Basics

According to the National Institute of Health, the pH of most of our crucial cellular and other body fluids like blood is designed to be at a pH of 7.4 which is slightly alkaline.

(You will also find resources pointing to 7.365 or near).

The body has an intricate system in place to maintain that healthy, slightly alkaline pH level no matter what you eat. This is an argument that many alkaline diet skeptics use, and I get it. It's 100% true, and I say the same thing.

This is not the goal of the alkaline diet. We just can't make our blood's pH more alkaline or "higher." Our body tries to work hard for us to help maintain our ideal pH. We can't have a pH of 8 or 9. If we did, we would be dead. It's not about magically raising your pH.

The focus of the alkaline diet is to give your body the nourishment and healing tools that it needs to MAINTAIN that optimal pH almost effortlessly.

If we fail to do so, we torture our body with incredible stress! Yes, when the body has to continually work overtime to detoxify all of the cells and maintain our pH, it finally succumbs to disease.

Let me name a few examples of what can happen if we continuously eat an acid-forming diet (also called SAD - Standard American Diet) and drink too much caffeine and sugar that does not support our body at all. Our body ends up sick and tired of working overtime and may manifest one or more of the following conditions:

- Chronic inflammation

- Immune and hormonal imbalance

- Lack of energy, mental fog- and you go for another cup of coffee yet still feel the same

- Yeast and candida overgrowth

- Digestive damage

- Weakened bones. Our body is forced to pull minerals like magnesium and calcium from our bones to maintain the alkaline balance it needs for constant healing processes.

In summary, eating more alkaline foods, for example veggies, herbs, and greens, helps support our body so that it can work for us at optimal levels, while eating more acidic food (aka processed food, fast food etc.) doesn't help at all. The alkaline diet is not about magically raising our pH, but about helping our body rebalance itself by supporting its natural healing functions.

Why is it called an alkaline diet, then?

To be honest, I don't know. It could also be called the Eat More Veggies Diet, or perhaps Veggie Lover Diet, but then most people would never even look at it. I guess that it was called the alkaline diet for a reason, probably to make it more mysterious and sexier so that there is this "hook" that makes people think, "Hmmm, what is it? That stuff must be hot!"

The alkaline diet is sisters with the Clean Food Diet, Anti-Inflammatory Diet, Vegetarian Diet, Vegan Diet, Macrobiotic Diet, and the Raw Food Diet. In fact, it offers an incredible blend and the best of them all. All those diets that are more in the plant-based category. If you want to learn more about the alkaline diet, get food lists etc. I warmly invite you to join my Alkaline Wellness Reader Newsletter.

As soon as you join, I will send you three exclusive bonus PDF eBooks (including alkaline plant-based desserts).

Also, by signing up to my newsletter, you will stay up to date with my latest book releases. (Whenever I publish a new book or course, you will be able to get them at a special launch price.) There's also contests, giveaways, new sexy recipes, motivation and other fun stuff to help you on your wellness journey to the best of my ability:

To join my newsletter, visit the link below:

www.HolisticWellnessProject.com/alkaline

(Please note- the best way to sign up is from your phone, tablet or PC. The eBooks I want to send you as a gift when you sign up are not available anywhere else and will be delivered to you via email, as a PDF. These are not kindle eBooks.).

Questions? - > email us at: info@holisticwellnessproject.com

Link to sign up to my Alkaline Wellness Reader Newsletter:

www.HolisticWellnessProject.com/alkaline

Alkaline Green Smoothies- How to Use This Book

If you have any health condition or allergy, be sure to double check with your doctor. Get the full list of foods and ingredients you can't have.

Then, when going through this guide, you can:

Focus only on the recipes that don't use those ingredients,

Or use any recipe you want but entirely skip the ingredients you can't have or replace them.

In most cases, skipping one or two ingredients in a recipe will not make a huge difference (unless we are talking about crucial components of the recipes, then you will need to replace that ingredient with something similar).

Example- coconut milk can be replaced with almond milk or any plant-based milk, or even water.

Grapefruit can be replaced with lemons.

Kale can be replaced with spinach.

Shall you have any questions or problems, please email us:

info@holisticwellnessproject.com

so that I, or someone from my team will get back to you to lend you a hand. We are always very happy to help our readers.

So, you don't need to stress out at all.

Oh, and if you are new to some superfood like chia seeds, moringa powder etc, most of those can be easily found online. I buy most of mine via Amazon. It's easy and fast.

The alkaline diet is not a diet but a lifestyle.

One of the best ways to embrace this lifestyle is to focus on adding more alkaline smoothies into your diet.

While most diets focus on counting calories and being restrictive, the alkaline diet focuses on abundance and enriching your diet with nutrient-rich alkaline foods.

As soon as you focus on that and get rid of the *I need to be perfect* mindset, you will start creating amazing long-term results, like having more energy, feeling happy and vibrant.

Now, let jump into the recipes.

I highly recommend you set a goal of having one massive green smoothie a day. At the same time, reduce caffeine, drink plenty of fresh water, focus on eating clean and you will soon start experiencing the miracle of a simple, healthy lifestyle.

Important

This is a simple to follow recipe and lifestyle book to inspire and motivate you on your wellness quest. However, it is not meant to diagnose or treat any medical conditions.

If you are suffering from any chronic disease, have recently undergone any medical treatment, are pregnant, lactating or suffering from any serious health condition, you need to speak to your doctor first.

It is also recommended that you familiarize yourself with all the precautions that the extended use of certain herbs entails. Some herbs may interfere with certain medications, and so if you take any, be sure to seek a professional advice first.

The Truth about Green Smoothies

An interesting fact is that green is not always alkaline...

For example, kiwis are green. However, they are not considered super alkaline forming because of their sugar content. And so, a kiwi smoothie, even though it's green, rich in fiber and vitamin C and definitely better for you than a chocolate bar, is not considered super alkaline.

The alkaline diet encourages you to reduce sugar and make about 70-80% of your diet rich in alkaline foods.

The same rule can be applied to smoothies. We need to focus on alkaline fruits (fruits low in sugar) and veggies to the best of our ability. The best example of alkaline fruits are: limes, lemons, grapefruits, pomegranates. They are low in sugar and full of alkaline minerals.

After that, it's fine to add some other fruit to make our smoothies taste great.

But- first of all we need to focus on alkaline ingredients.

Green tea is not alkaline either (even though it's green and good for you and full of antioxidants etc.) That is because the alkaline diet encourages you to stay away from caffeine, theine and other stimulants and focus on staying energized in a natural way.

And again, it's not about being 100% alkaline.

Balance is key and I have based the smoothie recipes from this book on that rule.

At the same time, not all green ingredients may be for you.

If you suffer from any allergies or are on medication that may interfere with certain foods, be sure to take note of that.

Aside from that- listen to your body and observe your digestion.

Even the most alkaline superfoods may just not be for you because everyone is different so take your personal preferences into consideration.

There are plenty of recipes in this book to pick and choose from. It's totally fine to pick just a few to begin with. Stick with what you like and what's easier for you.

This journey should be fun and we need to eliminate the resistance the best we can!

Measurements Used in the Recipes

The cup measurement I use is the American Cup measurement.

I also use it for dry ingredients. If you are new to it, let me help you:

If you don't have American Cup measures, just use a metric or imperial liquid measuring jug and fill your jug with your ingredient to the corresponding level. Here's how to go about it:

1 American Cup= 250ml= 8 fl.oz.

For example:

If a recipe calls for 1 cup of almonds, simply place your almonds into your measuring jug until it reaches the 250 ml/8oz mark.

Quite easy, right?

I hope you found it helpful. I know that different countries use different measurements and I wanted to make things simple for you. I have also noticed that very often those who are used to American Cup measurements complain about metric measurements and vice versa. However, if you apply what I have just explained, you will find it easy to use both.

Now, let's get into the recipes, that's why we are here, right?

Recipe Preparation

Most of the recipes I create and share are designed for busy people who are looking for fast solutions. With every new book, I want to make it even simpler and faster.

In alignment with that, there is no complicated preparation involved (although I'll admit, I have been guilty of that in some of my earlier books).

Precautions

I have already mentioned that the recipes in this book are not designed for self-medication or the treatment of any chronic diseases.

They are simple wellness and self-care recipes that form a part of a healthy, balanced lifestyle, in addition to a balanced diet.

I can certainly help you with inspiration, recipes, motivation and lifestyle tips.

However, any serious medical conditions must be discussed with your doctor.

Part 3 Alkaline Green Smoothie Recipes

Recipe #1 Kale and Cashew Smoothie

This is an amazing, creamy smoothie that is just perfect on a hot, sunny day. It offers refreshment and sneaks in lots of good greens. One of the best smoothies for beginners as the taste is very balanced. Yes, we use fruit to our advantage! At the same time, ginger adds to its anti-inflammatory properties and helps stimulate the lymphatic system. Maca is a natural energy booster and hormone rebalancer.

Serves 1-2

Ingredients

- ½ cup of fresh pineapple chunks
- 2 cups cold unsweetened cashew or almond milk
- 1 cup of kale leaves, washed and chopped
- ½ teaspoon maca
- ½ teaspoon cinnamon powder
- 2-inch fresh ginger, peeled
- ½ cup of crushed ice

***Optional: a few fresh mint leaves to garnish*

Instructions

1. Place all the ingredients (except ice and powdered ingredients) through the blender.
2. Now, open the blender and add the ice and powdered ingredients.
3. Blend again.
4. Pour into a smoothie glass, garnish with fresh mint and enjoy!

Recipe #2 Green Dream Smoothie

This is one of my favorite breakfast smoothies. It combines natural protein from chia seeds, good fats from coconut oil and of course- the healing greens.

We are spicing it up with some cherries to make it taste delicious!

Lime will help wake up your senses first thing in the morning. At the same time, it's an amazing addition to the iron obtained from spinach (and helps in better iron absorption)

This smoothie first thing in the morning will help you unleash all your superpowers, creativity and unstoppable energy.

Serves 1-2

Ingredients

- 2 cups cold unsweetened coconut milk (or any other plant-based milk that suits your needs)
- 2 tablespoons of chia seeds (or chia seed powder)
- ½ cup of cherries, pitted
- ½ cup of spinach, washed
- 1 lime, peeled and sliced
- Half avocado, pitted
- 1 tablespoon coconut oil

Instructions

1. Place all the ingredients in a blender.
2. Blend until smooth.
3. Pour into a glass and enjoy!

Recipe #3 Anti-Oxidant Quit Coffee Smoothie

People always ask me how to quit or reduce coffee.

Well, this recipe is perfect to help you make a transition without feeling like a blanched vegetable and without experiencing headaches and migraines (can happen as a caffeine withdrawal syndrome).

This smoothie uses a bit of matcha powder that is a better alternative to coffee. Although the alkaline diet in its ideal design does not use any forms of caffeine, it's not about being perfect. It's about progress. This recipe helps you do just that, and it tastes delicious while offering you a myriad of nutrients.

Serves: 1-2

Ingredients

- 1 green apple
- 2 cups coconut milk (use 1 cup if you want to make a thick, yoghurt like smoothie)
- 1 avocado, washed, peeled and pitted
- A few broccoli florets, washed and chopped
- Handful of frozen blueberries
- 1 teaspoon matcha powder

Instructions

1. Place all the ingredients in a blender.
2. Blend until smooth.
3. Pour into a glass and enjoy!

Recipe #4 Apple Carrot Mint Superfood Smoothie

This smoothie not only offers amazing refreshment and is beginner-friendly but it's also jam packed with a superfood-moringa. It's one of my favorite green powders and can be purchased online very inexpensively.

It works very well if you don't have any fresh greens at hand and want to give your smoothie that extra edge.

Moringa is an alkaline superfood. It contains all the essential amino acids – the building blocks of protein that are needed to grow, repair and maintain cells. At the same time, it's very rich in alkaline forming minerals such as magnesium, iron and potassium. To be honest, it tastes a bit "hardcore". That is why we are softening up this smoothie with a natural sweetness from apples and carrots.

Mint not only adds to its original sweet like taste, but it also helps with digestion while adding to the anti-oxidant and anti-bacterial properties of this amazing smoothie.

Serves 1-2

Ingredients

- 1 green apple
- 3 big carrots
- 1 cup coconut or almond yoghurt (plant-based)
- 1 cup coconut or almond milk
- 1 inch of fresh ginger, peeled
- 2 teaspoons moringa powder
- A handful of fresh mint, washed

Instructions

1. Place all the ingredients into a blender
2. Pour over the milk and yoghurt.
3. Blend well.
4. Enjoy!

Recipe #5 Spirulina Pineapple Flavored Protein Smoothie

This smoothie is an amazing recipe if you crave something sweet and creamy. And this is exactly what we are getting thanks to the creaminess of blended cashews (yum!) that offer us a ton of natural protein to keep us full and satisfied. At the same time, we are using that smoothie to sneak in some fresh greens and...we are spicing it up with nutrient dense spirulina powder.

We are using a bit of pineapple fruit to taste. Perfect balance!

Serves 1-2

Ingredients

- 1 teaspoon of spirulina
- A few slices of pineapple
- 1 ½ cups of unsweetened coconut milk
- 2 handfuls of raw cashews (unsalted)
- ½ cup spinach
- 1 teaspoon cinnamon powder to garnish

Instructions

1. Place spirulina, pineapple, cashews and spinach in a blender.
2. Pour in the coconut milk.
3. Blend well.
4. Serve in a smoothie glass and sprinkle some cinnamon powder on top (extra sweetness)

Recipe #6 Avocado Softness Morning Smoothie

This smoothie is a perfect breakfast smoothie. It incorporates good fats (from avocado) and vitamin C from limes to help you boost your immune system. Greens spice it up with some chlorophyll (this is a green smoothie book, so we no longer need to explain what the greens are doing here). Plus, natural protein from almonds and some light sweetness from green apples make this smoothie whole and complete. Just like we feel after drinking it.

Serves 1-2

Ingredients

- 1 ripe avocado, peeled, pitted and sliced
- ½ cup fresh kale leaves, washed
- 2 small limes, peeled and sliced
- 1 big green apple
- Handful of almonds (soaked overnight)
- 2 cups almond milk

Instructions

1. Place all the ingredients in a blender.
2. Pour over some almond milk.
3. Blend and enjoy!

Recipe #7 Cocoa Almost Alkaline Smoothie

While this smoothie is not strictly alkaline (cocoa is not considered alkaline), it surely is a Perfect Treat Smoothie. It's yummy and focuses on blending different superfoods so that you can still get the benefits of squeezing in some fresh greens!

Serves 1-2

Ingredients

- 2 tablespoons cocoa powder
- 2 tablespoons chia seed powder
- A few dates, pitted
- Half cup baby spinach, washed
- 2 cups creamy coconut milk, unsweetened
- Optional: stevia and cinnamon powder to sweeten

Instructions

1. Place all the ingredients (except cinnamon and stevia) in a blender.
2. Blend well, ensuring that the greens are well processed (unless you enjoy them sticking around your teeth).
3. Place in a smoothie glass.
4. If needed, sweeten with stevia and sprinkle over come cinnamon.
5. Enjoy!

Recipe #8 Energy Boost Creamy Smoothie

This recipe combines the freshness and an abundance of Vitamin C from grapefruits with iron coming from the greens.

Maca powder helps rebalance hormones, and cashews add to the creamy texture while making sure you also get in some protein and good fats to help you stay full longer.

Serves 1-2

Ingredients

- 1 large grapefruit, peeled and chopped
- 1 ½ cups of unsweetened coconut milk
- 1 tablespoon maca powder
- Handful of arugula leaves, washed
- Handful of fresh spinach leaves, washed
- Optional- a few dates to taste

Instructions

1. Place all the ingredients except dates in a blender.
2. Process until smooth.
3. Now, try the smoothie to see if you like the taste.
4. If needed, add in a few pitted dates and blend again.
5. Place in a smoothie glass, drink and enjoy!

Recipe #9 Refreshing Barley Grass Smoothie

While not everyone enjoys drinking pure barley grass, it's an amazing addition to a smoothie that is made up of delicious ingredients. Oh Marta, but why use green powders? Isn't it better to use fresh greens?

I always say- whenever possible, go for fresh. No need to use any powders if your kitchen is full of fresh greens and other produce ready to get blended. However, let's face it. Some days you may find yourself pressed for time. Or you may be lacking some ingredients. That is why it's always good to have some green powders, just in case. This smoothie uses barley grass powder. You could also use moringa powder, or any other green powder blend. I have a short overview of different powders on my blog, you can look it up for extra reference:

www.HolisticWellnessProject.com/greens

Serves: 1-2

Ingredients

- 1 to 2 teaspoons of barley grass powder
- ½ cup of frozen raspberries
- ½ cup frozen blueberries
- 1 lime, peeled
- Handful of cilantro leaves, washed
- Handful of mint leaves, washed
- 1 ½ cups of almond milk

Instructions

1. Place all the ingredients in a blender.
2. Process until smooth.

Recipe #10 "Almost Green" Green Smoothie

This smoothie is highly alkaline, because all its ingredients are highly alkaline-forming.

Beets, grapefruits, avocado, cucumber and greens.

Beets add natural sweetness, and aside from that help you boost your immune system with vitamin C. Grapefruits add more vitamin C and precious alkaline minerals such as potassium as well as a myriad of anti-oxidants. Cucumber is very refreshing and blends very well with other ingredients. Avocado adds in some good fats and hemp seeds offer natural protein.

Serves: 2-3

Ingredients

- 2 tablespoons hemp seeds
- 2 cups rice milk
- ½ teaspoon vanilla
- ½ cup of beets, peeled and chopped
- ½ cup collard greens
- 1 grapefruit, peeled and chopped
- 2 small cucumbers, peeled and chopped
- 1 small avocado, peeled, pitted and sliced

Instructions

1. Place all the ingredients in a blender.
2. Process well until smooth.
3. Serve and enjoy! You may also try it with some ice cubes.

Recipe #11 Apricot Delight Green Smoothie

This recipe is an excellent smoothie for beginners, who perhaps need to "mask" the taste of greens with other ingredients.

Apricots are an excellent source of vitamin A as well as vitamin C, copper, dietary fiber and potassium (which is an alkaline mineral).

Oranges add more Vitamin C and "orangeness" and finally, some fresh arugula leaves come in since it's their party (it's a green smoothie book, not an orange smoothie book).

Serves: 1-2

Ingredients

- ½ cup of fresh, dried or canned apricots
- 1 big orange, peeled and sliced
- 1 cup fresh arugula leaves, washed
- 1 cup coconut milk
- Half cup coconut water
- Optional: a few drops of liquid chlorophyll

Instructions

1. Place all the ingredients in a blender.
2. Blend well until smooth.
3. Serve in a smoothie glass and enjoy!

Recipe #12 Papaya Digestive Blend

Papaya contains many beneficial enzymes and has a high antioxidant content. Because of that it strengthens the immune system, helps the digestive system and protects against free radicals. That is why, we decided to "call her" to join the party for this alkaline green smoothie recipe that can be served as a meal replacement.

Serves: 2-3

Ingredients

- ½ cup fresh, green papaya, chopped
- 1 small avocado
- 1 small cucumber, peeled and chopped
- 1 green apple, peeled and chopped
- 1 cup coconut milk
- 1 cup water
- Handful of fresh cilantro leaves
- 2 tablespoons chia seeds

Instructions

1. Place everything in a blender.
2. Process until smooth, and feel free to experiment with the consistency by adding more water, if needed.
3. Serve and enjoy.

Recipe #13 Watermelon Green Smoothie

What a lovely mix! Watermelons are very hydrating, offer natural sweetness and are super refreshing.

We are spicing it up with some fresh parsley leaves.

Parsley is a highly alkaline forming ingredient, an excellent of vitamin K and Vitamin C as well as a good source of vitamin A, and iron.

Serves: 2-3

Ingredients

- 1 cup of watermelon, peeled and chopped
- 1 cup parsley leaves, washed
- 2 cups almond milk
- A handful of almonds, soaked overnight

Instructions

1. Place all the ingredients in a blender.
2. Process well until smooth.
3. Enjoy!

Recipe #14 Sweet Dreams Green Smoothie

This smoothie is designed to help you unwind in the evening (or whenever you want), so that you can enjoy deep, holistic relaxation, a better quality of sleep and feel amazing.

Serves:1- 2

Ingredients

- 1 cup boiling water
- 2 chamomile tea bags
- 1 cup gluten free oat milk
- Half cup dark leafy greens of your choice (kale, spinach, collard greens)
- Half a banana
- 1 teaspoon cinnamon powder
- 2 tablespoons of fresh mint leaves (1 is for the tea and 1 for the smoothie)

Instructions

1. Using a teacup or a teapot, combine the boiling water, 1 tablespoon mint leaves and 2 chamomile tea bags.
2. Cover and set aside.
3. In the meantime, place the leafy greens, banana, and 1 tablespoon of mint leaves in a blender.
4. Pour over the oat milk. Process until smooth.
5. Now mix the smoothie with the chamomile-mint infusion. Make sure the infusion is slightly warm, but not hot. Stir well. If needed, stir in more cinnamon powder. *Serve and enjoy. Sweet dreams!*

Recipe #15 Very Berry Greenness Smoothie

It's always a great idea to have some frozen fruit, ready to grab for a refreshing, anti-oxidant smoothie like this one!

Serves 1-2

Ingredients

- ½ cup of fresh or frozen raspberries
- 1 cup of cold coconut milk
- ½ cup of kale, washed and chopped
- Half an avocado, pitted
- A few slices of lime (set 1 aside to garnish)
- ½ cup of blueberries
- Optional: 1 teaspoon organic spirulina powder

Instructions

1. Blend all together and enjoy!
2. Serve in a smoothie glass and garnish with a slice of lime.
3. If you decide to use spirulina and are new to it, try to do a mini test first, to see whether you like the taste of it in your smoothie.

Recipe #16 Light Greenness Smoothie

This is another example of a simple yet highly alkaline-forming smoothie that can be made quickly and very inexpensively.

Cucumbers are real alkaline super foods that are very often overlooked. Yet, they offer vitamin C, vitamin A as well as alkaline minerals such as magnesium, potassium and manganese.

If you want to have a break from fruit smoothies, or are simply looking for something different out there, you will love this recipe.

You can also use it as a meal replacement or make it in a thicker version and serve it as a soup.

Serves: 1-2

Ingredients

- 2 big cucumbers, peeled and sliced
- 1 clove of garlic, peeled
- 1 cup coconut milk or yoghurt, unsweetened
- A few slices of avocado
- Pinch of black pepper
- Pinch of Himalayan salt
- Handful of fresh cilantro leaves, washed
- 1 tablespoon chia seed or hemp powder

Instructions

1. Place in a blender and process until smooth.
2. Serve in a smoothie glass as a smoothie, or in a small soup bowl.
3. If you go for the latter, my suggestion would be to serve it with a bunch of finely chopped raw veggies added into it. An amazing meal idea for a hot summer day.

Recipe #17 Ginger Anti-Inflammatory Smoothie

This smoothie is an excellent natural remedy for inflammation and helps boost the immune system.

Whenever I am feeling like I might be getting a cold or a flu, I resort to this smoothie to give my body what it needs to stimulate healing.

I also drink it on a regular basis during the winter.

Serves 1-2

Ingredients

- 2-inch ginger, washed and peeled
- 2-inch turmeric, washed and peeled
- ½ cup of arugula leaves
- 1 big grapefruit, peeled and chopped
- 1 cup coconut water

Instructions

1. Place everything in a blender and process until smooth.
2. Serve in a smoothie glass and enjoy!

Recipe #18 Sweet Herbal Mint Smoothie

What I love about avocados in my smoothies is that they are multifunctional. You can use them both in spicy veggie smoothies as well as in sweet, herbal smoothies like this one.

Fennel tea is one of my favorite herbal teas. It's good to help you alleviate anxiety, sleep better and also helps stimulate metabolism and fight off colds and flu. I know, it sounds too good to be true. But this is what super herbs like fennel are known for.

Serves 1-2

Ingredients

- ¼ cup of fresh mint
- 1 cup fennel tea (use 1 or 2 fennel tea bags per 1 cup of boiling water), cooled down
- 1 big ripe avocado
- A few dates, pitted
- Optional: some plant-based milk of your choice.

Instructions

1. Place the fresh mint, avocado and dates in a blender.
2. Pour over some fennel tea.
3. Blend well, and taste.

   If you are looking for a creamy taste, you can add in half cup of coconut or cashew milk of your choice. Enjoy!

Recipe #19 Mineral Beauty Green Smoothie

This smoothie recipe uses rooibos tea which will help you boost your energy naturally, so that you don't have to reply on coffee. rooibos is considered an alkaline tea, because if its high mineral and antioxidant content. In fact, it's one of my favorite teas, and it appears quite often in my recipes, especially in my book Alkaline Teas. In this recipe however, rooibos blends with other healing ingredients to create an amazing, holistic, green alkaline smoothie.

Let's do this!

Serves: 2

Ingredients

- 1 cup of rooibos tea, cooled down
- ½ cup almond or coconut milk
- 1 small avocado, peeled and pitted
- A handful of fresh mint leaves, washed
- A handful of baby spinach leaves
- 1 green apple, peeled and chopped
- 2 dates, pitted
- 1 inch of ginger, peeled

Instructions

1. Blend and enjoy!
2. If you enjoy rooibos tea in your smoothies, make sure you always have some in your fridge so that it's ready to grab to make a mineral rich alkaline smoothie to help you stay energized naturally.

60

Recipe #20 Irresistible Veggie Smoothie

What I really love about veggie smoothies is that they can also be turned into a quick meal. It's a real time saver! At the same time, any veggie leftovers can be added into a smoothie.

Serves 2-3

Ingredients

- 1 tablespoon extra-virgin cold pressed olive oil
- A few broccoli florets, raw or cooked
- 1 cup of artichoke hearts, cooked
- 2 handfuls of greens of your choice
- Pinch of Himalayan salt
- 2 garlic cloves
- Pinch of black pepper
- 1 ½ cups raw cashew milk, unsweetened
- A few cilantro leaves to garnish (optional)
- A few onion rings to garnish
- Some water, if needed, to experiment with consistency

Instructions

1. Place in a blender.
2. Process until smooth.
3. Serve in a smoothie glass or a small soup bowl.
4. Garnish with cilantro and/or onion rings.
5. Enjoy!

Recipe #21 Spicy Pepper Smoothie

Another simple and tasty veggie smoothie that will keep you full for hours and can also be served as a nice filling soup. I really like this recipe as a quick lunch. It's just so easy to make it!

Serves: 2-3

Ingredients

- 2 green bell peppers, chopped
- 1 cup filtered water
- 1 cup coconut milk, unsweetened
- Handful of kale leaves, washed
- 2 chili flakes
- Pinch of Himalayan salt to taste
- Pinch of black pepper to taste
- 1 garlic clove
- Optional: 2 tablespoons chopped chives to garnish

Instructions

1. Blend all the ingredients adding some Himalayan salt and black pepper to taste.
2. Serve in a smoothie glass or a small bowl and garnish with some chives.
3. Enjoy!

Recipe #22 Cinnamon Almond Treat Smoothie

This smoothie is an amazing and refreshing alkaline-forming green smoothie you can turn to whenever you are craving something sweet. Its good fats and natural protein from almonds will keep you full for hours.

Serves 1-2

Ingredients

- 2 teaspoons of cinnamon powder
- 1 cup almond milk
- 1 tablespoon coconut oil
- A handful of mint leaves
- Half avocado, peeled and pitted
- Optional: shredded coconut and some raisins to garnish

Instructions

1. Blend and enjoy!
2. Serve in a smoothie glass or a dessert bowl, with a spoon.
3. Sprinkle over some shredded coconut and/or some raisins.
4. If needed sprinkle some more cinnamon powder and if you want to go a bit crazy with this one, sprinkle over some cocoa powder too.

Recipe #23 Healing Ashwagandha Anti-Stress Smoothie

Ashwagandha is known as an adaptogenic herb. Adaptogens are substances such as amino acids, vitamins and herbs that modulate the body's response to stress and/or a changing environment, both of which are consistent aspects of modern-day life.

Adaptogens are known to help the body cope with and fight against external stressors such as toxins and the environment, as well as internal stressors such as anxiety, insomnia and depression.

In this recipe, Ashwagandha blends with other healing ingredients to offer an amazing and super relaxing evening smoothie.

Serves: 1-2

Ingredients

- 1/2 teaspoon of Ashwagandha powder
- 1 cup oat milk
- 1 small lime
- Half avocado
- ¼ cup shredded coconut

Instructions

1. Blend everything together until smooth.
2. Serve in a smoothie glass and enjoy!

Recipe #24 Green Gazpacho Smoothie

This recipe is a variation of the original Spanish gazpacho recipe in a super green super food version.

It can also be served as a refreshing soup.

Serves: 2-3

Ingredients

- 4 medium sized cucumbers, peeled and chopped
- 1 big garlic clove, peeled
- 2 tablespoons extra-virgin, cold pressed olive oil
- 1 ½ cups filtered water
- Pinch of Himalayan salt
- Pinch of black pepper

Instructions

1. Place all the ingredients in a blender and process until smooth.
2. Serve in a smoothie glass and enjoy!
3. If you prefer to enjoy this recipe as a soup, you can garnish it with some chopped chives and other raw veggies (like red and green bell peppers).
4. Enjoy!

Recipe #25 Healing Green Factory

Here comes another delicious veggie smoothie recipe.

Celery is a very alkaline forming ingredient. It is rich in vitamin C, fiber, alkaline minerals such as potassium and is also very hydrating and replenishing.

Perfect for a simple, green super alkaline smoothie.

Serves 1-2

Ingredients

- ½ cup of celery
- 1 tablespoon virgin, cold pressed olive oil
- Pinch of Himalayan salt
- ½ teaspoon apple cider vinegar
- 1 teaspoon of chia seeds
- 1 cup coconut vegan yoghurt, unsweetened
- 1 small avocado
- Pinch of black pepper to taste
- A few fresh cilantro leaves to garnish

Instructions

1. Place all the ingredients in a blender and process until smooth.
2. If needed season with Himalayan salt and black pepper.
3. Serve in a smoothie bowl or glass and garnish with some fresh cilantro leaves.

Recipe #26 Lime Energy Boost Smoothie

This is a super simple alkaline green smoothie that will help you boost your immune system by enriching your diet with vitamin C and a myriad of alkaline minerals.

It's very refreshing and easy to make too!

Serves 1-2

Ingredients

- 2 big limes, peeled
- 1 cup of coconut or almond milk
- A handful of kale leaves, washed
- 1 kiwi, peeled
- Optional- a few drops of liquid chlorophyll
- 1 lime wedge to garnish (1 per serving)

Instructions

1. Place in a blender.
2. Process until smooth.
3. Serve in a smoothie glass and garnish with a wedge of lime.
4. Enjoy!

Recipe #27 Arugula Revolution Smoothie

If you happen to have any arugula salad leftovers, this smoothie recipe will help you turn them in a truly delicious, alkaline green smoothie experience. Maca and chlorella will help you boost your energy naturally.

Serves 1-2

Ingredients

- ½ cup of arugula leaves, washed
- 1 orange, peeled and cut into smaller pieces
- 1 pear, peeled and cut into smaller pieces
- 1 ½ cups almond milk
- A handful of almonds, soaked overnight
- Half teaspoon maca powder
- Half teaspoon chlorella powder

Instructions

1. Place all the ingredients in a blender.
2. Process until smooth.
3. Serve in a smoothie glass and enjoy!

Recipe #28 Smooth Relaxation Smoothie

This smoothie is one of my favorites ones to unwind with. Especially if you get to enjoy it in a nice, warm aromatherapy bath!

Serves: 1-2

Ingredients

- ½ avocado, peeled and pitted
- ¼ cup of shredded coconut
- 1 cup oat milk
- ½ teaspoon of vanilla

Instructions

1. Place in a blender.
2. Process until smooth.
3. Serve in a smoothie glass and if you want, enjoy this smoothie in a nice relaxing bath!

Recipe #29 Optimal Refreshment Balance Smoothie

This smoothie recipe combines antioxidants from blueberries with the optimal hydration from watercress as well as a myriad of vital nutrients from moringa green powder.

Serves 1-2

Ingredients

- ½ cup of blueberries
- ¼ cup of watercress
- 1 cup of almond milk
- 1 teaspoon moringa green powder
- A few mint leaves to garnish

Instructions

1. Place all the ingredients in a blender.
2. Process until smooth.
3. Serve in a smoothie glass and garnish with mint leaves.
4. Enjoy!

Recipe #30 Creamy Green Protein Smoothie

This smoothie is perfect as a quick refreshing snack that sneaks in a ton of good superfoods!

It can also be served as a soup.

Serves 1-2

Ingredients

- 1 cup of fresh vanilla dairy-free vegan yogurt
- 6 tablespoons green peas
- 2 cucumbers, peeled and chopped
- Half an avocado, peeled and pitted
- ½ iceberg lettuce
- A few green onion rings
- 1 garlic clove, peeled
- A pinch of Himalayan salt to taste
- A pinch of black pepper to taste
- 1 tablespoon sweet red pepper powder to garnish

Instructions

1. Place all the ingredients (except the red bell pepper) in a blender.
2. Process until smooth.
3. Taste to see if you need to add some salt.
   Serve in a bowl and sprinkle over some black pepper.
   Sprinkle over some sweet red pepper powder and enjoy!

Recipe #31 Oil Yourself UP Comfort Smoothie

This recipe uses hemp oil which is great to re-balance hormones, soothe anxiety and improve the mood.

The delicious blend of sweet potatoes and spices makes it a perfect comfort smoothie.

Serves 1-2

Ingredients

- 1 big sweet potato, peeled and cooked
- 1 tablespoon of hemp oil
- 1 cup coconut milk
- Half an avocado, pitted and peeled
- A handful of cilantro leaves, washed
- A handful of parsley leaves, washed
- Pinch of Himalayan salt
- Pinch of curry powder
- Optional (if you like it spicy) a pinch of chili powder

Instructions

1. Place all the ingredients in a blender.
2. Process until smooth.
3. Taste to check if you like to taste or if you need to add a bit more of Himalayan salt or curry powder
4. Serve in a smoothie glass, or a bowl and enjoy!

Recipe #32 Simple Warm Mint Smoothie

This is a very simple herbal smoothie recipe that can be served as chilled or slightly warm, depending on your preferences.

This smoothie is great for digestion and relaxation.

Serves 1-2

Ingredients

- 1 teaspoon of mint leaves
- ½ cup of almond milk
- ½ teaspoon of fresh vanilla
- ½ cup chamomile infusion, cooled

Instructions

1. Place almond milk, mint leaves and vanilla in a blender.
2. Process until smooth.
3. Pour into a smoothie glass and mix it with chamomile infusion (warm or cold, depending on your preferences).
4. Enjoy!

Recipe #33 Beauty Smoothie Revolution

This smoothie combines the alkalinity and beta-carotene of carrots and tomatoes with the alkalinity and "greenness" of moringa powder and cilantro.

Good fats from avocado and coconut oil will help you stay full longer and prevent sugar cravings. It will help you have a glowing, healthy looking skin too! All this while helping your body get back to balance.

Serves 1-2

Ingredients

- 1 tablespoon coconut oil
- 1 cup of cashew or other nut milk of your choice
- 2 small carrots, peeled
- 2 mid-sized tomatoes, washed (optional- you can peel them)
- Handful of fresh cilantro leaves, washed
- 1 teaspoon moringa powder

Instructions

1. Place all the ingredients in a blender.
2. Process until smooth.
3. Pour into a smoothie glass, stir well, serve and enjoy!
4. For optimal results, drink this smoothie 4-5 times a week.

Recipe #34 Protein Pea and Carrot Smoothie

This smoothie can be also served as a nice soup (warm or cold).

Serves: 2-3

Ingredients

- ½ cup of peas, washed
- 2 carrots, peeled and chopped
- A handful of fresh parsley leaves, washed
- 1 garlic clove, peeled
- Half cup raw cashew milk
- Half cup water, filtered
- Himalayan salt to taste

Instructions

1. Place all the ingredients in a blender.
2. Process until smooth.
3. Serve in a smoothie glass or a bowl.

Enjoy cold or slightly warm.

Recipe #35 Almond, Flaxseed Green Protein Smoothie

The flaxseed meal is an excellent source of Omega-3 fatty acids, aka "good fats". Good fats are also found in almonds, so this smoothie is packed full of both healthy fats and protein. After having this smoothie, not only will you feel full and satisfied but you will also get an energy boost!

Serves: 1-2

Ingredients

- 15-20 almonds
- 1 big peach, washed and pitted
- 1 cup of almond milk,
- 2 teaspoons of flaxseed meal
- A handful of fresh baby spinach, washed
- Optional: 1 teaspoon fresh moringa powder

Instructions

1. Place all ingredients in a blender.
2. Blend until combined and almonds are blitzed.
3. Serve into a chilled glass and enjoy!

Tip: Add a small amount of water or coconut water (fantastic after workouts) if you want a thinner smoothie.

Recipe #36 Super Alkaline Spicy Veggie Smoothie

This smoothie is an excellent energy boosting veggie protein smoothie. Perfect as a quick lunch or whenever you need an energy boost. I love it in winter, since it's so spicy it helps me stay warm.

Sometimes, I like to serve it as a warm soup with some quinoa in it. Whatever you decide to choose, the possibilities are endless!

Serves:1-2

Ingredients

- 1 cup coconut milk
- ½ cup of fresh red bell pepper, washed and chopped
- ½ cup of fresh green bell pepper, washed and chopped
- Half an avocado, peeled and pitted
- 2 chili flakes
- 2 tablespoon cold pressed, virgin olive oil
- A handful of fresh arugula leaves
- 1 tablespoon of hemp seeds
- 1 tablespoon chia seeds
- Himalaya salt to taste

Instructions

1. Place all the ingredients in a blender.
2. Process until smooth.
3. Season with Himalayan salt to taste.
4. Serve and enjoy!

Recipe #37 The Green Factory Smoothie

This superfood smoothie recipe combines a myriad of powerful greens to help you look and feel amazing. Spinach is packed full of iron (more than you will find in a T-bone steak) and has also been found to work as a natural appetite suppressant. Celery is a great source of fiber and B vitamins and will contribute to the prevention of water retention. Cucumber is also packed full of fiber and B vitamins and will join the fight against water retention. Dubbed "the beauty food", watercress is the secret weapon in this green machine, protein-packed smoothie. Watercress is the leader of anti-aging vegetables, with enormous amounts of vitamin K and other healthy nutrients that contribute to healthy skin, hair and nails.

Serves: 2-3

Ingredients

- ½ cup spinach
- 1 cucumber, chopped
- ½ cup of celery, chopped
- ½ cup of fresh watercress
- 2 cups of cashew or coconut milk
- 1 tablespoon coconut milk
- Pinch of Himalayan salt to taste, if needed

Instructions

1. Add all ingredients to a high-powered blender and processed until well blended. Enjoy!

Recipe #38 Pumpkin Green Soup Smoothie

This is another amazing and powerful veggie blend to help you conjure up an alkaline green smoothie that will help you feel energized and full for hours.

Serves: 1-2

Ingredients

- 1 cup of almond milk
- ½ cup of organic pumpkin puree
- ½ cup broccoli florets (raw or cooked)
- 1 tablespoon of organic almond butter
- ½ teaspoon of nutmeg powder
- Small handful of hemp seeds (optional)
- Himalayan salt to taste

Instructions

1. Add all ingredients to a blender.
2. Blitz until well combined.
3. Pour into a glass and serve as warm or chilled.

Recipe #39 Almost Green Superfood Treat

This superfood smoothie packs a protein punch as well as providing an array of benefits from the different superfoods used in the recipe. It will keep you energized for most of the day and will help fight off those mid-morning cravings

Goji berries contain a great number of antioxidants that help to give you healthy skin and protect the eyes. They also help to boost your immune system. They also provide a source of complex carbohydrates which will ensure you have a sustained release of energy, helping you to keep active throughout the entire day.

Serves:1-2

Ingredients

- 1 ½ cups of coconut milk
- 1 sweet potato, peeled and cooked
- Half cup baby spinach, washed
- 2 tablespoon of cacao nibs
- 1 teaspoon of maca powder
- 2 tablespoons of flaxseed meal
- 1 tablespoon of chia seeds
- 1 teaspoon of hemp seeds
- 1 teaspoon of vanilla extract
- A small handful of goji berries, to garnish

Instructions

1. Add all the ingredients into a high-powered blender.
2. Blitz until well combined.
3. Pour into a chilled glass.
4. Sprinkle goji berries or other fruits on top and serve.

Recipe #40 Sunflower Green Energy Smoothie

This smoothie offers a balanced mix of fruits and veggies as well as natural protein and good fats.

Serves: 1-2

Ingredients

- 1 cup of hazelnut milk (or any other nut milk of your choice)
- 4 tablespoons desiccated coconut
- Half cup pomegranates
- Half cup iceberg lettuce
- 1 grapefruit
- A handful of fresh parsley
- 2 tablespoons sunflower seeds

Instructions

1. Add all ingredients into a high-powered blender.
2. Blitz until well combined.
3. Pour into a chilled glass, garnish with fruits of your choice and serve.

Bonus Recipes- Delicious Alkaline Smoothie Bowl Recipes

The following bonus recipes will inspire you to start turning some of your smoothies into delicious and creative smoothie bowls.

Smoothie bowls are amazing as a quick breakfast or a guilt free snack. They can be sweet or sour.

They will help you add a ton of healing superfoods into your diet.

Enjoy!

Bonus Recipe #1 Anti-Inflammatory Smoothie Bowl

This smoothie offers a unique combination of vitamin C and anti-inflammatory, highly-alkalizing ingredients like ginger and turmeric. It's especially recommended for winter and fall because it helps boost the immune system to prevent flu and colds.

If you dread the idea of including raw spinach leaves in your smoothie bowl, have no fear. Spinach and oranges are an excellent combo, not only because orange will help neutralize the taste of the spinach, but also because the vitamin C from the oranges (or any other vitamin C-rich foods, I am not saying it must be oranges) helps in iron absorption.

Serves: 1-2

Ingredients for the Smoothie

- A handful of fresh spinach
- 1 orange
- 1 one-inch piece of ginger root, peeled
- ½ teaspoon turmeric
- 1 cup rice or coconut milk

More Ingredients for the Toppings:

- Handful of blueberries
- A few fresh mint leaves
- 2 tablespoon crushed almonds or almond powder

Instructions

1. Blend all the ingredients until smooth. If you are making this smoothie on a hot summer day, feel free to add some ice cubes. Pour into a bowl.
2. Add the rest of the ingredients on top.
3. You can enjoy your smoothie bowl now or store it in the fridge for later.

To learn more about the healing power of turmeric (and how to add it into your diet), I recommend you check out the following article (very detailed + recipes) on my blog:

www.holisticwellnessproject.com/turmeric

Bonus Recipe #2 From the Sea Bowl

Another option for a not-so-sweet smoothie! It offers a myriad of nutrients such as B vitamins and iodine from nori and Omega-3s from chia seeds. With some green veggies like zucchini and kale, you are bound to alkalize your body quickly and feel energized the way you deserve!

Serves: 1-2

Ingredients

- 2 nori sheets, soaked
- 1 cup coconut water
- ½ avocado
- 1 small zucchini
- Handful of kale (thick stalks removed)
- 1 teaspoon flax seeds
- 1 teaspoon chia seeds
- 1 tablespoon almond butter
- 1 tablespoon ground almonds
- Himalayan salt to taste

More Ingredients for the Toppings

- Handful of pistachios
- Handful of crushed cashews
- 1 slice of lemon

Instructions

1. Blend all the ingredients until smooth. If you are making this smoothie on a hot summer day, feel free to add some ice cubes. Pour into a bowl.
2. Mix in the rest of the ingredients by placing them on top. Enjoy!

Bonus Recipe #3 Super Energy Creamy Smoothie Bowl

This is an incredible smoothie with a creamy consistency and energizing ingredients. It's perfect for moments of mental and physical stress. Packed with Vitamin B6, potassium, and copper, it will help you alkalize your body. Maca is an amazing hormone balancer, particularly for women. Cinnamon and cacao are great mood boosters for me and add to the feeling of comfort and coziness.

Serves: 1-2

Ingredients for the Smoothie

- 1 cup chestnut milk
- 1 cup almond milk
- 1 teaspoon maca powder
- 1 teaspoon raw cacao powder
- ½ teaspoon cinnamon
- Handful of ice (optional)
- ½ tablespoon coconut oil

More Ingredients for the Toppings

- 2 tablespoons of coconut cream or coconut yogurt
- Handful of blueberries
- 2 slices of lime

Instructions

1. Blend all the ingredients until smooth. If you are making this smoothie on a hot summer day, feel free to add some ice cubes. Pour into a bowl.
2. Mix in the rest of the ingredients. First, sprinkle the coconut cream or yogurt on top of the smoothie and then top it with blueberries and garnish with lime slices.
3. You can enjoy your smoothie bowl now or store it in the fridge for later.

Bonus Recipe #4 Super Green Bowl

Chlorophyll is the secret power of alkalinity. All you need to do is create a habit of adding a few drops of liquid chlorophyll to your smoothie bowls. You can also use powdered chlorophyll or even green powder mix that contains different alkaline herbs. For example, Organifi is a blend created by a well-known health expert Drew Canole. It can be a great solution if you want something you can throw into your smoothie bowls that offers an all-in-one solution. It will depend on your personal choices and lifestyle because Organifi contains matcha, and matcha is a stimulant. If you are caffeine-intolerant, it may not be for you. You can still use chlorophyll or any other green powder, for example moringa, which is one of the ingredients in the Organifi blend.

I suggest you visit:

www.HolisticWellnessProject.com/greens

On our website, we do our best to help you learn more about different supplements to make sure you choose something that will work for you.

Serves: 1-2

Ingredients

- 1 handful of baby spinach leaves
- 4 tablespoons fresh mint leaves
- 1 cup of rice milk
- 1 teaspoon chlorophyll powder (or a few drops of liquid chlorophyll), or 1 teaspoon of Organifi green powder blend

- ¼ cup blueberries
- ½ apple

More Ingredients for the Toppings

- Handful of sunflower seeds
- Handful of hemp seeds
- 1 slice of lemon or lime
- A few dates (pitted) or raisins
- A few grapes

Instructions

1. Blend all the ingredients until smooth. If you are making this smoothie on a hot summer day, feel free to add some ice cubes. Pour into a bowl.
2. Mix in the rest of the ingredients by placing them on top.
3. You can enjoy your smoothie bowl now or store it in the fridge for later.

Bonus Recipe #5 Sweet Potato Alkaline Smoothie Bowl

Most people fear carbohydrates, but when it comes to healthy carbs, there is nothing to fear. They will help you start the day feeling energized and happy. This is also a fantastic pre-workout recipe where sweet potatoes are the primary ingredient! With some added Omega-3 and protein from the flax seeds and green super-alkaline ingredients, you will have an incredible and tasty breakfast or snack.

Serves: 1-2

Ingredients

- 1 cup cooked sweet potatoes, peeled and chopped
- 1 cup of almond or coconut milk (unsweetened)
- ¼ teaspoon nutmeg
- ¼ teaspoon ground cinnamon
- 1 teaspoon flax seed
- One small avocado
- A few spinach leaves
- Optional: ½ teaspoon moringa powder

More Ingredients for the Toppings

- Handful of crushed almonds
- Handful of crushed cashews
- 3 tablespoons fresh orange juice

Instructions

1. Blend all the ingredients until smooth. If you are making this smoothie on a hot summer day, feel free to add some ice cubes.
2. Mix in the rest of the ingredients by placing them on top.
3. You can enjoy your smoothie bowl now or store it in the fridge for later.

Bonus Recipe #6 Creamy Guilt-Free Protein Bowl

Raspberries are back in the game again alongside some creamy and delicious ingredients and natural protein. If you are still feeling skeptical and thinking, "How do I get protein on a plant-based diet?" Well, fear not. In this smoothie bowl, not only will you get protein, but also taste, alkalinity, and energy! Enjoy.

Serves: 1-2

Ingredients

- 1 cup frozen raspberries (keep a few for decoration)
- 1 cup coconut yogurt (natural, no added sugar). You can also use coconut cream or thick coconut milk. If you are allergic to coconut, any plant-based yoghurt (or dairy) will do here, so don't worry.
- 1 tablespoon chia seeds
- A handful of baby spinach
- 1 orange
- 1 small avocado

More Ingredients for the Toppings

- Handful of crushed almonds
- Handful or grapes
- 2 tablespoons almond or coconut powder

Instructions

1. Blend all the ingredients until smooth. If you are making this smoothie on a hot summer day, feel free to add some ice cubes.
2. Mix in the rest of the ingredients by placing them on top.
3. You can enjoy your smoothie bowl now or store it in the fridge for later.

Bonus Recipe #7 Mediterranean Anti-Inflammatory Mix

If you like Mediterranean flavors and spices, you will love this. Who said smoothie bowls must be sweet? Also, this one is super alkaline! It is a fantastic lunch idea. Even people who don't usually like veggies like this smoothie bowl, at least according to my experiments and volunteers.

With a creamy, healthy, filling, alkaline avocado base, the flavors are added to with some glorious fresh herbs that bring these vegetables to life!

Serves: 1-2

Ingredients

- 1 avocado
- 1 cup coconut milk, unsweetened
- ¼ cup mixed herbs like oregano, mint, and parsley
- Juice of 1 lemon
- 3 tomatoes
- 1 cucumber
- 1 tablespoon cashew nut butter
- 10 green olives
- A few spinach leaves

Ingredients for the Toppings

- Handful of pistachios
- Handful of black olives
- 1 slice of lemon
- A few basil leaves

Instructions

1. Blend all the ingredients until smooth. If you are making this smoothie on a hot summer day, feel free to add some ice cubes. Pour into a bowl.
2. Mix in the rest of the ingredients by placing them on top.
3. You can enjoy your smoothie bowl now or store it in the fridge for later.

Part 4 Extra Alkaline Diet Tips & Suggestions to Help You on Your Journey

Let's finish off this book with my best tips to help you look and feel amazing.

When you combine the following tips with the recipes and empowering mindset from this book, you will be able to dive deep, transform your body and mind and feel amazing.

Here are a few simple guidelines that will help you transition towards a healthy, alkaline lifestyle. These are compatible with different nutritional lifestyles (Gluten Free, Vegetarian, Vegan) and it's totally up to you what you choose to focus on:

Eliminate processed foods from your diet and say "no" to colas and sodas

There are so many additives and preservatives in these foods. They have been known to create hormone imbalances, make you tired, and add to acidity in your body. It's just not natural for humans to consume those conveniently processed foods.

The label may even say "low in calories or low in fat"- it will not help you in your long-term weight loss or health efforts. In order to start losing weight naturally, your body needs foods that are jam-packed with nutrients. Real foods. Living foods. This, in turn, will help your body maintain its optimal blood pH almost effortlessly.

Add more raw foods into your diet

Especially lots of vegetables and leafy greens as well as fruits that are naturally low in sugar (for example, limes, lemons, grapefruits, avocados, tomatoes, and pomegranates are alkaline forming fruits).

Reduce/eliminate animal products

These are extremely acid-forming. The good news is that there are many plant-based options out there and tons of way to create delicious alkaline-friendly plant-based meals you will love! If I could do it, you can do it too.

Drink plenty of clean, filtered water

Preferably alkaline water or alkaline fruit-infused water (lemons, grapefruits, limes and pomegranates are great for that)

Add more vegetable juices into your diet

These are a great way to give your body more nutrients and alkalinity that will result in more energy, less inflammation and, if desired, natural weight loss.

Vegetable juices are the best shots of health! I have also written a book called *Alkaline Juicing* if want to give it a try and want to juice the right way.

Reduce/eliminate processed grains, "crappy carbs" as well as yeast (very acid-forming).

Personally, I recommend quinoa instead (it's naturally gluten-free), amaranth (very nutritious), brown rice, or soba noodles (they're made from buckwheat and naturally gluten-free).

You can also use gluten-free wraps or make your own bread. Fruit is also a great natural source of carbohydrates, and great for energy. Plus, they always make a great snack!

Reduce/eliminate caffeine

Trust me - it will only make you feel sick and tired in the long run and can even lead to adrenal exhaustion (not the best condition to end up in - I have been there).

It may seem a bit drastic at first, and yes, I know what you're thinking- there are so many articles out there praising the benefits of caffeine and coffee.

Yes, I am sure there are, as many people build their business around coffee. This is why there must be something out there that promotes it. At the same time, I agree that everything is good for you in moderation.

As long as you have a healthy foundation, you can have coffee as a treat (I do drink coffee occasionally).

There is no reason to be too strict on yourself. But...don't rely on caffeine as your main source of energy. Green tea may be helpful too as a transition, but green tea is not caffeine-free either so don't overdo it.

On the other side of the spectrum - green tea is rich in antioxidants and a great part of a balanced diet, so it's not that you have to get paranoid about all kinds of caffeine. Moderation is the key.

Try to observe your body. Personally, I have noticed that quitting my coffee habits (I used to have 2-3 coffees a day) and replacing coffee with natural herbal teas and infusions has really made my energy levels skyrocket.

Now I sleep better, and I get up feeling nice and fresh. I don't need caffeine to keep me awake. I no longer suffer from tension headaches and I feel calmer.

Yes, I do have a cup of coffee as a treat sometimes, usually when I meet with a friend, but I no longer depend on it. I choose it; it doesn't choose me.

Think about this and how you can apply this simple tip to your life to achieve total wellbeing. Coffee and caffeine in general are extremely acid-forming. I recently started using an Ayurvedic herb called Ashwagandha. It is known as an adaptogenic herb and it can help you restore your energy levels naturally.

I highly recommend you give it a try.
I have also written a book called *Alkaline Teas*. It's all about healing, herbal, alkaline friendly infusions that will help you get your energy naturally so that you don't need to depend on caffeine. In this book, we go deeper into no caffeine drinks.

Replace cow's milk with almond milk, coconut milk or any other vegan friendly milk

For example, quinoa milk, chia seed milk, oats milk-whatever works for you and your stomach that works well for you.

Cow's milk is extremely acid forming and personally, I don't think it makes sense for humans to drink milk that is naturally designed for fattening baby calves not humans.

Quitting dairy was one of the best things I have done for myself. I have noticed that even very little milk would cause digestive problems and it was really easy to fix-I quit drinking milk.

I also learned about cruelty in the dairy industry which obviously contributed to my decision. The best thing about the alkaline plant-based diet is that you can still have ice cream and other treats- you just make them with no milk/animal products. It's so much healthier and tastier, totally guilt-free.

With this approach, there is no need to go hungry or be deprived.

You focus on an abundance of foods and meals that are good for you, delicious and such a choice is also better for the animals and the planet. This is what I call "holistic motivation".

Don't fear good fats- coconut oil, olive oil, avocado oil etc.

These alkaline oils are good for you and should replace processed margarines, and artery-clogging trans-fats. This is not to say that you can "drink" them freely. Balance is the key. **Use stevia instead of processed sugar and Himalayan salt instead of regular salt**

Stevia is sweet but sugar-free and Himalayan salt contain some amounts of calcium, iron, potassium and magnesium plus it also contains lower amounts of sodium than regular salt.

Add more spices and herbs into your diet- not only do they make your dishes taste amazing, but they also have anti-inflammatory properties and help you detoxify (cilantro, turmeric, and cinnamon are miraculous).

As you can see, the alkaline diet is a pretty common-sense clean diet. Nothing is exaggerated. Nothing is too strict. Nothing is too faddish. Eat more living foods and avoid processed foods. Try to eat more plant-based foods. Don't reject it before you have tried it.

Add regular relaxation techniques to the alkaline diet (including yoga, meditation), time spent in nature, adequate sleep and physical activity (we need to sweat out those toxins) and you have a prescription for health.

It's strange to me that there are so many people putting the alkaline diet down, however, the general guidelines I have mentioned above are common sense for a healthy lifestyle and I am sure your doctor would agree with it (more natural foods, less processed crap, more relaxation, less stress).

This is the gist of the alkaline diet lifestyle. This is what will make you feel nice and rejuvenated and achieve your ideal weight. The problem is that some people are not willing to take those small commonsense steps and are looking for a "secret formula"- something that will magically help them with no effort at all. I am not judging- I have been guilty of it as well. We all have!

The truth is that whatever changes you want to make in your life (this rule applies not only to health) can be hard as leaving one's comfort zone is difficult, but with time and practice it becomes easy and automatic.

Holistic success is about applying what we already know and using the information to better our lives. This is what I call "the secret formula." <u>Information in action</u>. I always say that I am very open-minded when it comes to different diets. I never claim that what I do is the only path to wellness and health. I prefer to provide you with information and inspiration so that you can create your own way and choose what works for you. Everyone is different.

You need to learn to listen to your body and be good on yourself.

Conclusion

Thank you once again for taking an interest in my book.

I am really grateful for you, and I hope you were able to pick at least a few recipes you will enjoy.

My mission is to empower and inspire you to live a healthy lifestyle so that you can become the best version of yourself while enjoying the process of your transformation.

Let's finish the book with a motivational kick:

The Benefits of Alkaline Green Smoothies and Hydration:

•By adding natural drinks to your lifestyle, you will be able to stimulate natural weight loss and reduce unhealthy sugar cravings. You see, when you take care of your hydration, especially with alkaline smoothies and natural drinks, your body is also getting a myriad of nutrients and so it doesn't have to send you those "feed me I am so hungry" signals all the time.

•You will feel more energized for sure as your body is able to flush out toxins more quickly. Think how all areas of your life can change if you have more energy!

•Your mental and emotional health will improve with a well-hydrated body, allowing you to think better and perform better.

•You will get a ton of extra vitamins and minerals.

•Your skin will be clearer and feel smoother.

•Your cardiovascular health will be optimized.

+ You will feel stronger, and a totally new person.

So next time you feel tempted to drink something unhealthy, ask yourself, "Is it worth it? Or maybe I can choose a nutrient-packed alkaline smoothie?"

It's all about making consistent progress and about those small daily decisions.

They will help you create what I like to call *empowering alkaline mini habits*. These, when compounded, will help you to transform in a way you never even thought was possible. It will be an amazing experience.

Finally, I need to ask you for a small favor. It will only take a few minutes of your time and will be very helpful for me at this stage. All I am asking you for is your honest review on Amazon. Your review, even a short one, can inspire someone else to start living a healthy lifestyle and enjoy the benefits of alkaline hydration.

Let's make a world a happy, healthy and more empowered place.

That collective transformation starts with small baby steps and micro-actions.

Thank you, thank you, thank you. I am really looking forward to reading your review.

Be sure to visit the next page and follow my instructions to be notified about my new books and start receiving more valuable tips about the alkaline diet & lifestyle to help you stay on track.

Xxx   *Marta*

Let's Keep in Touch + Free Alkaline Wellness Newsletter

Picture this...whenever Marta releases a new book, you receive an email from her and are the first one to be notified.

Not only that, but you are also able to get her new books at a discounted price (up to 50%), take part in awesome giveaways (the last one we did was a super cool juicer), be the first one to get notified about her courses and get access to private videos, bonus recipes and other awesome trainings to help you stay on track and live an alkaline lifestyle without feeling deprived.

"Sounds great, but what do I need to do?"

It's a very simple process. All you need to do is to visit Marta's private website below:

www.HolisticWellnessProject.com/email

Be sure to use your phone, PC or a tablet.

If you use your kindle device, you may get stuck with this process. So, visit:

www.HolisticWellnessProject.com/email

and join Marta's newsletter now. As a welcome gift, you will receive three free bonus alkaline eBooks.

Be sure to reply to Marta's first email and say hi 😊

OK, enough of writing about myself in the third person.

I am looking forward to connecting with you,

Marta Xxx

Marta's Work – Holistic Wellness, Mindfulness & Alkaline Diet

I have written dozens of wellness, recipe and holistic lifestyle guides, books and articles.

I am also very active at creating online courses as it allows me to be a coach to many beautiful souls from different locations at the same time.

You will find all my work at:

-www.HolisticWellnessProject.com (books, articles, audio's)

-www.AlkalineDietLifestyle.com (courses & programs)

-www.amazon.com/author/mtuchowska (Amazon Kindle, paperback & Audible publications)

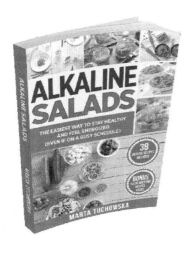 

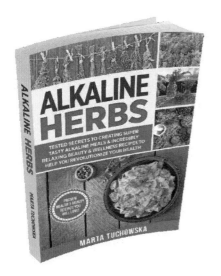

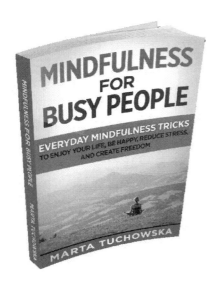

Printed in Great Britain
by Amazon

55055292R00066